Healthy
Desserts

Published by Blue Dome Press
535 Fifth Avenue, Ste. 601
New York, NY 10017-8019, USA

www.bluedomepress.com

Art Director Engin Çiftçi
Graphic Design Nihat İnce
Photographs Semih Ural

ISBN: 978-1-935295-46-4

Printed by
İmak Ofset, Istanbul - Turkey

Healty Desserts

with Natural Sweeteners

M. Ömür Akkor

BLUE DOME

New York

Contents

Healthy Desserts from World Cuisine

Acknowledgments

I would like to express my appreciation to my sister, Zennup Pınar Çakmakcı, and her husband, Ramazan Çakmakcı, for guiding me to write this book, to Hakan Doğan, Ayhan Doğan, and Dilek Doğan for always having recipes, and for making and trying them, to Sevim Üstünbostancı and Özlem Aktürk, who did not grudge to provide photos, to Semih Ural, who vitalized the recipes with pictures, and to my family, for all their efforts.

M. Ömür Akkor

Introduction

What is Sugar?

Sugar is an organic chemical substance in the carbohydrate group. Commercially, it can be obtained from plant sources. Since sugar is produced from carbon dioxide and photosynthesis from water, it can be made from all green plants. Sugar is naturally found in honey, milk, fruit, and various vegetables. Purified carbon hydrate consumed under the name sugar is from molasses, sugar cane, and sugar beet, the major sources of refined sucrose. Since 350–400 BCE, sugar has been produced from sugar cane. But we consume much more sugar than our ancestors, who ate fruit and honey instead.

The production of sugar from the sugar beet, the most popular source, has taken place since the 19th century. Sugar produced from sugar cane brought to a standstill the production of sugar from sources such as honey, dates, maple, and other similar sources. It is important not to confuse refined sugars such as sucrose, dextrose (grape sugar) and fructose, which are procured with techno-chemical methods and sold alongside sugar procured from natural means. Sugar procured either naturally or chemically is called sugar. In the eyes of chemists, sugar is the general name of a broad class of various organic compounds.

Dessert Consumption

Nearly all mammals have a sweet tooth. A determinant of that is the fact that milk is sweet. Researchers on infant nourishment have ventured that an inclination toward sweet food is innate to humans, even a born addiction. Senses such as sweet, salty, and sour are implicit in the structure of the tongue.

However, in this century, it is very easy and inexpensive to get sugar. Today, many communities consume sugar in great amounts. People approach the concept of dessert as an indispensable thing, and decorate each happy moment with desserts. Birthdays, anniversaries, and holiday feasts following Ramadan are some examples. In the eyes of most people, very sweet foods are very delicious. But the habit of consuming refined, chemically produced sugar has reached a dangerous stage for our health. Alternatives for refined sugar must be explored.

Short History of Sugar

Deciding not to consume sugar requires vigilance and continuous effort today. Sugar has become so common that we find it everywhere, and in everything. Truly, it was hard to imagine this world even a few centuries ago. In Europe by end of the 17th century, sugar was consumed from restricted agricultural production in limited areas for an expensive price. The production and distribution of sugar together with coffee, tea, and cocoa were a significant part in the development of capitalism. These intermediary nourishments of the past were exotic and pleasing, and interest arose in places where they were distributed scarcely. Only lately was sugar used in daily life.

Historically, sugar was used in five ways: medicine, condiment, decorative, sweetener, and preserver. It was used as a nourishment substance after the 18th century. Though sweet dishes have always been part of our traditional cuisine, preparing these desserts with refined sugar is nearly new. In the Ottoman era, whitened sugar, not chemically refined, could be found in cities. But it was not able to replace molasses and honey. The popularity of tea, ubiquitous nowadays, was in process at the end of the 19th century.

The sugar of Ottoman cities bears no resemblance to the refined sugar produced so abundantly via technology, which is dangerous to our health. In the past, there were many kinds of sugar, including bleached white sugar, raw sugar, plant sugar with large clear crystals, unrefined red sugar, loaf sugar and others.

Health

We should approach sugar from a historical context, considering it an intermediary nutrient instead of a main nutrient. Unfortunately, in modern daily life, cheap, ubiquitous refined sugar is a main nutrient consumed daily. Refined sugar is not a food product.

Consuming this chemical stripped of all its benefits is truly dangerous for our health. It is inevitable that such consumption will create unhealthy communities. The current situation is even more fatal now, because sugar cane, the main source of sugar for ages, was replaced by sugar beet, which was replaced by sugar corn. The corn syrup found in most processed foods is very dangerous for our health, for it has the peculiarity of fattening almost fifty percent more than sugar made from the sugar beet. We can compare refined sugar to nicotine, by its impact on the human body. Sugar is a monster that destroys our health by reaching our cells immediately after the moment of consumption, providing us with instantaneous, short-lived energy, then leaving us hungry again, which causes our weight gain. Whenever a person uses nicotine, the passage of time leads to an inclination for ever increasing doses. Likewise, when a person eats refined sugar, he needs more and more to be satisfied. It is a vicious cycle; we must break the cycle by quitting sugar. Natural nutrients reach our cells only after a long process in the digestive tract. This food-processing system is necessary for our bodies to function well. For example, the sugar in honey and fruit is used only after a long procedure of digestion. Our bodies consuming sugar in food is very healthy. But we are facing a substance made from genetically modified corn, which uses shortcuts in our food processing system and quickly enters the walls of our cells, resulting in the spiking and crashing of our insulin levels, affecting even the neurotransmitters that provide communication between the neurons of the brain, making us addicts. We must distinguish this monster from natural, traditional sweets such as molasses, honey, maple syrup, etc. The major source of energy in our bodies is glucose. But glucose is not a substance obtained externally. Our bodies produce simple glucose from the intake of more complex natural foods. For instance, when we eat spinach, our bodies eventually turn it into glucose to produce energy. Therefore it is completely wrong to assert that a lack of refined sugar will mean a lack of energy, or that we need refined sugar for better brain functioning. The sugar industry tries to equate glucose and refined sugar in the minds of consumers. Calling every sweet thing sugar is a great barrier to distinguishing between healthy and unhealthy foods.

Healthy Desserts

The purpose of this book is to present to the reader a dazzling array of dessert recipes prepared without refined sugar. I compiled these traditional recipes from those of our ancestors, made with natural ingredients such as fruit, honey, and molasses, instead of refined sugars. In the battle of sugar addiction, natural desserts are going to be your closest helper.

Ours is a time of causing addictions and then earning money through those addictions. Such addictions like narcotics, gambling, alcohol, and nicotine work with the same reasoning. In these industries, there are sayings such as "Addict, sell, and earn" and "Make a healthy person unhealthy and sell him a medicine." Refined sugar is the most popular and greatest substance of addiction. Children in the past ate less harmful sweets. Obesity and other relevant health issues did not prevail in adults, let alone children. Therefore, humankind will be able to break this vicious cycle of addiction only by returning to the food of their forefathers.

Our aim is to overcome our addiction to refined sugar, an industrial product, by replacing unhealthy dessert recipes with healthy ones. The first stage of extricating oneself is quitting refined sugar and instead eating healthy sugar-free desserts. Later on, one can aim at decreasing dessert consumption in general. The healthiest thing for us is to eat food as close as possible to how they appear in nature.

These desserts, though they are made with natural ingredients, may still be dangerous for diabetics and people who suffer with similar illnesses. People on strict sugar-free regimens should not eat these desserts. People with weight issues should obey the advice of dieticians and nutritionists. **Everyone should approach this book with the knowledge that it is not a medical book but a dessert recipe book.**

Is Every Sweet Made of Sugar?

Nowadays the concept of sugar is synonymous with sweetness. We have the illusion that sweet means sugar. Sugar is sweet, but not every sweet is made of sugar.

From a historic perspective, it is difficult to join the assertion of some academic circles which claim that even natural foods like honey and fruit should not be consumed, placing them in the same category refined sugar and foods that our forefathers used for ages. Humankind obtained vitamins and minerals from fruit and honey for thousands of years. In our struggle against industrial and addictive sugar, honey and fruit are natural replacements for us and our children.

Sweet dishes have been around for centuries, and are part of our cultural cuisine. There were times when sugar was too expensive to be popular, and it could not find consumers in Anatolia. But an immense dessert culture was always present, and natural sources of sugar were used; but the modern popular usage of refined sugars has brought our dessert culture to the verge of extinction.

With this book we hope to improve general knowledge on the subject of remembering and protecting traditional desserts, part of our rich Turkish cuisine, by compiling desserts that are still prepared, with those about to be forgotten. Desserts made with honey, molasses, dried fruit, fruit juices, neroli oil, and other similar natural sources that contain no refined products such as white sugar and fructose, are termed sugar-free desserts.

God bless the hands of the cooks, and bon appetite to those who eat them.

Important Points While Preparing Desserts

General Rules:

- Oven should be preheated.
- All ingredients must be fresh.
- Flour must be sifted for almost all desserts.
- Pay attention to differences in degrees of home and industrial ovens, for there may be 10- to 20-degree Celsius differences between them.
- Dessert making requires weighing ingredients. While preparing desserts it is necessary to have scales.

Rules for Preparing Pie:

- For making a good pie dough all ingredients used must be cold. Pay attention to it. Remove all ingredients from fridge before getting started. Add flour and salt at least 30 minutes after their being cooled.
- For making good pie dough, knead it lightly. It should be quickly kneaded and rolled out. If butter remains in dough in pieces, then it will be crispy and delicious.
- For the dough's being much better and delicious, it is very important to let it wait in the fridge for 1 hour after making it and for 40 minutes after placing it into pie pan.

Rules for Preparing Cake:

- All ingredients required for preparing cake should be at room temperature.
- Ingredients should be removed from the fridge an hour before.
- Flour should be sifted.
- Oven should be preheated.

- After placing a cake into the oven, the door should not be opened during the first 25 to 30 minutes.
- Baking will proceed from the outer to the inner. In order to check the readiness of cake, you may insert a toothpick. If the toothpick comes out clean, the cake is ready.
- Cake should not be taken from the oven right away. It should be left for a while in an oven with an open door.
- Cakes can be cut only after letting them cool for at least 20 minutes. This will help cakes to get doughy.
- If you are going to use cream cheese, then you should primarily soften it by blending. The cream should be ready before the cake is.

Rules for Preparing Cookies:
- If you replace 10 percent of the flour used for preparing cookies with cornstarch or hazelnut flour, then your cookies will be melt in your mouth.
- Cookies must be baked in preheated ovens.
- Look at the bottoms of cookies to check their readiness. If the dough changed color to golden-brown, they are ready.

About Usage of Honey and Molasses:
- Honey can be found anywhere, but this is not true for molasses, which is found only at local markets. For desserts you may use real, unrefined, natural maple syrup or genuine fruit syrups instead of molasses.
- When honey and molasses were used in desserts, it was usually the last step, except for in cakes.

Table of Measurements

Honey and Molasses

1 cup honey or molasses = 250 g (≈ 8.8 ounces)

1 tablespoon honey or molasses = 20 g (≈ 0.7 ounces)

Flour

1 cup flour = 140 g (≈ 4.94 ounces)

1 tablespoon flour = 9 g (≈ 0.3 ounces)

Cacao

1 teaspoon cacao = 9 g (≈ 0.3 ounces)

1 teaspoon of cacao = 4 g (≈ 0.14 ounces)

Cornstarch

1 cup cornstarch = 140 g (≈ 4.94 ounces)

1 tablespoon cornstarch = 9 g (≈ 0.3 ounces)

Baking Powder

1 teaspoon baking powder = 4 g (≈ 0.14 ounces)

Baking Soda and Salt

1 teaspoon baking soda (or salt) = 4 g (≈ 0.14 ounces)

Yogurt

1 cup yogurt = 170 g (≈ 6 ounces)

1 tablespoon yogurt = 15 g (≈ 0.5 ounces)

Butter

1 cup butter = 225 g (≈ 7.93 ounces)

1 tablespoon butter = 15 g (≈ 0.5 ounces)

Water or Milk

1 cup water = 250 g (≈ 8.5 ounces)

1 tablespoon water = 15 g (≈ 0.5 ounces)

Eggs

1 egg (unshelled) = 55 g (≈ 1.94 ounces)

Yolk of an egg = 20 g (≈ 0.7 ounces)

Egg white of an egg = 35 g (≈ 1.2 ounces)

Cream

1 cup cream = 235 g (≈ 8.3 ounces)

1 tablespoon cream = 15 g (≈ 0.5 ounces)

Pistachios

1 pound pistachios = 453 g (≈ 16 ounces)

1 tablespoon pistachios = 9 g (≈ 0.3 ounces)

Walnut

1 pound walnut = 453 g (≈ 16 ounces)

1 tablespoon walnut = 9 g (≈ 0.3 ounces)

Hazelnut

1 pound hazelnut = 453 g (≈ 16 ounces)

1 tablespoon hazelnut = 9 g (≈ 0.3 ounces)

Coconut flakes

1 cup coconut flakes = 50 g (≈ 1.76 ounces)

1 tablespoon coconut flakes = 5 g (≈ 0.17 ounces)

Peanut

1 cup peanut = 453 g (≈ 16 ounces)

1 tablespoon peanut = 11 g (≈ 0.38 ounces)

Strained Palatial *Ashura* (Noah's Pudding)

In the Ottoman era, *ashura* earned the title of the "Palatial Dessert." In 1870, the dessert prepared by Pertevnial Sultan, mother of Sultan Abdulaziz, by her own recipe was recorded as "Strained Palatial Ashura." On the 10th of Muharram, preparations that started in the kitchen days before would end only after the distribution of *ashura*. Long lines would form at the doors of the palace, as well as at the Yıldız Talimhane Square.

2 cups wheat	1 cup honey
10 cups water	5 tablespoons rosewater
½ cup dried apricots	2 cups milk
½ cup dried figs	¼ pound pine kernel
½ cup raisins	¼ pound crushed walnut
1 cup boiled garbanzo beans	¼ pound crushed pistachios
1 cup boiled butterbeans	¼ pound crushed hazelnuts
1 cup boiled broad beans (horse beans)	1 cup pomegranate seeds

(Since spices like musk and others are hard to find in modern conditions, this recipe was simplified.)

Soak wheat overnight in a deep bowl full of water. Boil wheat in a large pan. Wait until wheat gets thoroughly cooked, about 1 hour. Place the boiled wheat into a bigger pan with a strainer. Smash wheat pulp well and set aside. Finely chop dried apricot and fig. Boil dried apricot, fig and raisins separately for 5 minutes, then strain. Add garbanzo beans, butterbeans, broad beans, honey, rosewater and milk to a strained wheat pulp and cook them on low heat for 20 minutes. If water boils down, add some water for consistency. When *ashura* is nearly ready, add half of dried fruit and close the lid. Place *ashura* in individual cups, decorate with remaining dried fruit and pomegranate, and serve when cool. (You may also try *ashura* with molasses or maple syrup.)

Serves 10.

(Ashura is generally prepared for there to be too much and offered to the neighbors.)

Quince Stew

Quince Stew was one of the desserts particular to the hard times of the Liberty War in Bursa, where quinces are abundant. Used as a sweetener were cracked wheat and molasses, which were stored in a rice jar, and could be found in every home. The business of the skillful housewives of Bursa was to prepare this delicious treat with whatever they had on hand.

4 medium quinces
A slice of lemon
1 cup water
1 tablespoon of cracked rice
1 cup molasses
2 tablespoons butter

Peel quinces and remove their seeds. Cut into 2 halves and let them soak in a deep bowl, in lemon water, to preserve their original color. Set soaked quinces in a pan and add water. Add rice and cook for 20 minutes on low heat. When the dessert is nearly done, the water should be nearly gone. As soon as water is gone, add molasses and butter. Cook under a closed lid for a few minutes more, cut the heat and leave it to sit. As soon as it cools, serve plain or with sour cream as a garnish.

Serves 4 to 6.

Nin-da Tu

This dessert hails from the Hittites and is a kind of pudding. It is 4000 years old, and it has been almost completely forgotten in the modern age. The people of Çorum, who lived on the lands of the Hittites, used to call this dessert "malak." The residents of western Anatolia called it "mamalika," and some still prepare it.

1 cup water
1 cup flour
1 tablespoon of butter
1 cup molasses

Mix water and flour in a medium saucepan and start cooking them. As soon as water boils, the mixture will start hardening into a pudding. When pudding gets to the correct consistency, pour into individual bowls. Lightly melt butter and molasses in a small pan, then pour the syrup over the pudding.

Serves 6.

Pepeçura

This sweet was cooked most often in the Black Sea region where grapes, particularly Rize grapes, grew in abundance. Despite a plethora of Pepeçura recipes, from Rice Pepeçura to Flour Pepeçura to Raisin Pepeçura to Molasses Pepeçura, unfortunately, this dessert is not prepared anywhere other than the Black Sea region.

2 tablespoons cornstarch
½ cup water
3 cups red grape juice

Mix well starch and water in a bowl. Pour grape juice into a medium saucepan and start heating. When grape juice starts to boil, mix in starch and keep stirring. Continue cooking on low heat. When the mixture becomes consistent, pour into bowls or glass cups. As soon as it cools, decorate and serve.

Serves 6.

Kaygana

❧

Instead of the borrowed French word "omelette," our people used the word "kaygana" or "gaygana" more frequently. The egg dish used to be prepared with sugar, jam, minced meat, eggplant and parsley. Mustafa Ali, from Gelibolu (1541–1600), was a prominent poet, writer and historian who had written that kaygana could be made in many different ways and presented independently.

Kaygusuz Abdal, in the 15th century, mentioned "honey kaygana" in his poems. In recipes from the same century, kaygana was prepared with a thin sheet of dough, drenched in water and then immersed into beaten eggs. They were stacked in a tray and then fried. In recipes after the 18th century, there was no dough.

4 eggs

1 tablespoon flour

¼ cup milk

1 tablespoon butter

1 tablespoon honey

2 tablespoons molasses

A red fruit for serving

Crack eggs in a mixing bowl. Add flour and pour on milk. Mix well. Melt butter in a wide pan and pour in egg mixture. When it is cooked, place it on a wooden board and cut into 2 equal semi-circles. Then fold, or cut, and place 4 equal pieces on a serving plate. In a cup, mix honey and molasses. Put red fruit on *kaygana*, pour the honey-molasses mixture over it, and serve.

Serves 2.

Walnut Sweet Sticks

This is a typical Anatolian dessert prepared in this land for centuries. There are several narratives about its origin, and recipes that include all kinds of molasses and dried fruit.

The first-known record was found in Afyon in the 15th century. Evliya Çelebi (1611–1682), in his travel book, praised the walnut sweet sticks of Manisa, Eğriboz, and İstanbul. By the 19th century, nearly all the cities of Anatolia had differing names and recipes for this dessert.

2 pounds walnut halves

3 cups molasses

1 cup cornstarch

1 cup water

5 meters linen yarn

String the walnuts onto the yarn, leaving space after groups of 5. Cut spaces in between 5-walnut strands, and make sure there remains a bit of yarn to hold on each side. Pour the molasses into a large pan and let it boil. Meanwhile, mix well cornstarch and water in a bowl. Add it to the molasses. Stir constantly to prevent the mixture from getting lumpy. When molasses becomes condensed, turn off heat. Prepare a set-up for hanging the sweet sticks, such as a drying rack. Place a tray underneath where you will hang the sweet sticks. Dunk the stringed walnuts into the molasses, and promptly hang them up. The excessive molasses will drip onto the tray. Repeat until all the walnuts are done. If the molasses gets too thick, reheat it. If you want the sweet sticks to be thicker, repeat this procedure several times. Serve when cool. (You can make dried fruit roll-ups from the molasses left on the tray.)

Serves 10.

(You can keep this dessert in a jar or cloth for 6 months.)

Cezerye

❧

Cezerye is a dessert prepared near the Mediterranean Sea region since long ago. They say it came from Algeria (Jazair). "Jazar" is an Arabic word meaning "carrot."

1 pound grated carrots
1 cup honey
1 teaspoon allspice
1 teaspoon ginger
1 teaspoon cornstarch
½ cup water
1/3 pound peeled pistachios
Wax paper
¼ pound shredded coconut

Place carrots in a pan and let them sauté on low heat in their own water. 20 minutes later, add honey, allspice, and ginger. Stir constantly. Mix starch and some water and add to the sautéing carrots. When the mixture becomes pasty, add pistachios and remove from heat. Spread wax paper on a baking sheet. Sprinkle half of coconut on paper. Spread the prepared mixture on the coconut. Sprinkle the remaining part of coconut on top. When it gets cool, cut it as you wish.

(You may also prepare it with walnut and hazelnut.)

Serves 10.

(You can keep it in a cool place for a few months.)

Traditional Turkish Desserts
Rice Pudding *(Sütlaç)*

3 tablespoons rice
1 cup water
3 tablespoons cornstarch
5 cups milk
½ pound honey

Simmer rice for 20 minutes. Drain it but keep the drained water. Add cornstarch into drained water and blend well. Pour milk into a pan and let it boil. As soon as milk boils, add starch mixture and rice. Return to a boil for 2 more minutes, then remove from heat. Let dessert cool for a while. Add honey. Place in oven bain-marie style (in a water bath or double boiler), into heat-resistant cups. Bake under 200°C (392 F) until the pudding turns golden-brown on top. Cool and serve with crushed walnuts or hazelnuts, dried fruit, vanilla or other sweeteners.

Serves 6 to 8.

Dried Mulberry Pulp

6 pound white mulberries
2 ounces cornstarch
2 ounces flour
1 cup water
Linen cloth

Smash fresh mulberries, place in a large pan, and bring to a boil. Half an hour later, use gauze or cloth to drain mulberries into another pan. Reheat until it gains the consistency of molasses. As soon as it attains the consistency of molasses, mix starch, flour and water in a bowl, then add that mixture into the pan. This provides shining color and easy spreading. Remove from heat when it gets condensed. Spread a linen cloth on a table and pour the pulp. With the help of a spatula, make it a thin layer. Wait for a few days, until it hardens. When completely dry, remove it from cloth, roll it, and serve with any dried fruit. (Try this recipe with fruit such as grapes, apricots, and others.)

Serves 10.

(You can keep this dessert in a jar or cloth for 6 months.)

Govdun

This dessert is from Erzurum, a region in eastern Turkey known for mulberries and walnuts, especially when winter temperatures reach -15°C (5°F). Mulberries gathered in summer are dried. In winter, dried mulberries and walnuts are crushed finely in a mortar. *Govdun*, prepared frequently in winter, is a very important nourishment in the cold.

1 cup crushed walnuts
1 cup dried mulberries

Place walnuts and dried mulberries in a wide mortar. Keep crushing them until walnuts excrete oil and mixture become consistent. When the mixture turns into jelly, eat with a spoon, or serve it in the shape of cookies. If the old-fashioned mortar-and-pestle way of preparing this dessert tires you, first blend in a food processor before taking the mixture into the mortar.

Serves 4.

Apple *Baklava* with Olive Oil

4 apples, peeled and grated
1 cup chopped walnuts
1 teaspoon cinnamon
½ cup honey
½ cup olive oil
20 sheets phyllo dough
Molasses or maple syrup for serving

Drain grated apple well. Add walnuts, cinnamon, and honey. Set the mixture aside. Grease a baking tray with olive oil and set aside. Roll out the phyllo sheets and brush the upper sheet with oil. Spread the apple mixture on the oiled phyllo sheet, take it by the edge and roll it. Cut the rolled dough into 3 equal pieces, and place them on the tray. Repeat this process for all the phyllo sheets. Bake in a preheated 180°C (356°F) oven for about 20 minutes, or until top and bottom are golden. Serve baked *baklava* with molasses or maple syrup.

Serves 8.

Honey Curd *Baklava*

20 sheets phyllo dough
¼ pound melted butter
1 pound curd or risotto cheese
1 cup honey

Grease a baking tray. Brush a sheet of phyllo dough with butter, and place it into the tray. Repeat ten times. Sprinkle curd or risotto on stack of phyllo. Repeat second step ten more times. Carefully cut into squares and bake in a preheated 180ºC (356ºF) oven for 25 minutes. After it cools 10 minutes, generously and evenly pour honey over the *baklava*. When completely cool, serve.

Serves 8.

Pumpkin with Molasses

2 pounds chopped pumpkin
½ cup water
1 cup molasses

Put pumpkin and water in a medium saucepan, and simmer for half-hour on low heat. When pumpkin is about to boil down, add molasses and cook for 3 more minutes. Remove from heat. Let it sit for 30 minutes. Serve with sour cream, sesame seeds, chopped walnut, or all three. (You may substitute maple syrup for molasses.)

Serves 8.

Horis

❧

This dessert was prepared in Erzurum in times of war and poverty, with whatever was in the house. Besides being a dessert, horis was a superb choice for brunches.

¼ pound butter
½ cup flour
½ cup comb honey

Put butter and flour in a medium saucepan; stir continuously on medium heat. Continue to stir until flour turns light brown, about 15 minutes. When flour reaches desired color, remove from heat and add honey to the middle. Honey will melt from the residual heat. When the honey is melted, serve.

Serves 4.

Apricot Jam
with Molasses

1 ½ pound dried apricots
1 cup water
1 cup molasses

Cut apricots in small or large chunks. Place them in a medium saucepan with water over heat. Cook until water is gone (about 15 minutes). Add molasses and cook for 3 more minutes. Remove from heat. When it is still hot, it might seem consistent enough. It will become much more consistent as it cools. Do not overcook. Once it cools completely, store in a jar and serve anytime. (Try this recipe with other dried or fresh fruits.)

Serves 8.

Honey Curd Pear

4 pears, peeled
1 teaspoon butter
4 sticks cinnamon
½ pound curd cheese
½ cup milk
8 tablespoons molasses

Sauté pears with butter in a large saucepan. Add cinnamon. (If you want them very soft, then first boil the pears.) Place curd cheese and milk into a food processor and blend until creamy. On the bottom of a serving plate, pour the creamy mixture. Stir molasses into sautéed pears until coated, then remove from heat. Let pears sit a few minutes, then pour them onto the creamy mixture, and serve.

Serves 4.

Pistachio Puree with Honey

½ pound shelled and ground pistachio

1 ounce honey

Bagels or fried bread for serving

Fry pistachio lightly in a medium pan and cease the flame before they completely alter their color. Put them into a food processor and blend until the oil is extracted. Put pistachio butter onto a deep plate, and add honey gradually, spoon by spoon. Mix well with a wooden spoon. Stirring will make it cooler. As it cools, it will get thicker. Once cooled, serve with bagels or fried bread.

Serves 4.

Strawberries with Curd Cheese

1 cup curd cheese
½ cup milk
1 pound strawberries
2 tablespoons honey

Blend curd cheese and milk in a food processor until creamy. Spread this cream on bottom of serving bowls. Place strawberries randomly on cream. Decorate with honey and serve.

Serves 4.

Healthy Desserts from World Cuisine

Cookies with Walnuts

¹/³ pound finely chopped walnuts
2 ounces chopped hazelnuts
¹/³ pound honey
4 ounces egg whites

Mix all ingredients thoroughly in a deep bowl. Cook in a medium pan
for 5 minutes. Spoon walnut-sized pieces onto a baking sheet. Bake in
a preheated 180ºC (356ºF) oven for 7 minutes, cool and serve.

Serves 4 to 6.

Cookies with Fig

¼ pound dried figs

2 ounces crushed walnuts

2 ounces chopped hazelnuts

2 ounces honey

2 ounces egg whites

2 tablespoons coconut flakes

2 teaspoons cacao

½ teaspoon baking powder

½ teaspoon vanilla

Chop figs and walnuts very finely. Mix them with hazelnuts, honey, egg whites, coconut flakes and cacao in a large mixing bowl. Bake them in a large pan for 5 minutes. When it gets a bit cooler, add baking powder and vanilla. Bake all in a preheated 180°C (356°F) oven for 10 minutes. Cool for 20 minutes and serve.

Serves 4 to 6.

Hazelnut Grape Cake

❧

1 cup raisins
4 eggs
8 ounce honey
½ pound butter
1 pound flour
2 teaspoons baking powder
½ cup hazelnuts

Let raisins plump in a deep bowl full of hot water. Mix eggs, honey, and butter at room temperature until creamy in a large mixing bowl. Add flour and baking powder with a wooden spoon. Strain the raisins and add them into the mixture. On a well-greased baking sheet, place a layer of hazelnuts and shake so that the hazelnuts are stuck to the surface. Then pour cake mixture and bake at 180ºC (356ºF) for 45 minutes. Cool for 20 minutes and serve.

Serves 8.

Carrot Cake

2 eggs

4 tablespoons honey

¼ pound butter

4 ounces milk

1 ½ pound flour

1 teaspoon baking powder

2 carrots, grated

½ cup finely crushed walnuts

1 teaspoon cinnamon

Beat eggs well in a deep mixing bowl. In this order, add honey, room-temperature softened butter, milk, and flour mixed with baking powder. Beat the mixture thoroughly for 1 minute before adding each ingredient. Fold in grated carrots, walnuts, and cinnamon. Mix by hand with a wooden spoon or spatula. Pour the mixture into a greased cake tin or baking sheet, bake at 180ºC (356ºF) for 40 minutes. Cool for 20 minutes and serve.

Serves 8

Walnut Nougat

1 pound cream
1 pound honey
1 pound crushed walnut
1 tablespoon olive oil

Mix cream and honey in a deep pan and place over heat. Cook them on low heat for about 40 minutes by continuously mixing. First it will get watery, then it will thicken. When the mixture turns brownish in color, add walnuts and cook for 2 more minutes. Remove from heat. Grease a marble surface or heat-resistant table thoroughly with a tablespoon of olive oil and pour on nougat. Cool it by folding it with a spatula. Crush walnuts with a wooden spoon. After it completely cools, remove from the surface, cut and serve. (Nougat can also be an ingredient or decoration for other desserts.)

Serves 10.

Apricot Molasses Pie

Pie shell:

⅓ pound flour

¼ pound butter

3 tablespoons honey

1 tablespoon water

Filling:

2 ounce hazelnut powder

1 tablespoon honey

½ egg white of one egg

Topping:

1 cup apricots

½ cup molasses

Mix pie-shell ingredients in a mixing bowl. Wrap dough in stretch wrap and cool in fridge for an hour. While dough is cooling, mix filling ingredients in a mixing bowl and set aside. Roll dough out with a rolling pin. Spread it in a greased pie tin, twist the edge into a crust, and set aside. Pierce the pie dough with a fork several times. Again place the dough in fridge for a half-hour. Then bake the shell in a preheated 180ºC (356ºF) oven for 15 minutes. Cool.

Spread the filling in the cooled, baked pie shell. Place apricots however you wish. Bake again at same temperature for 10 minutes. Cool. Lightly pour warm molasses over pie and serve.

Serves 6 to 8.

Pear Almond Pie with Honey

Pie shell:

⅓ pound flour

¼ pound butter

3 tablespoons honey

1 tablespoon water

Filling:

2 ounce hazelnut powder

1 tablespoon honey

½ egg white of one egg

Topping:

2 pears

½ cup crushed almond

3 tablespoons honey

Mix pie-shell ingredients in a mixing bowl. Wrap dough in stretch wrap and cool in fridge for an hour. While dough is cooling, mix filling ingredients in a mixing bowl and set aside. Roll dough out with a rolling pin. Spread it in a greased pie tin, twist the edge into a crust, and set aside. Pierce the pie dough with a fork several times. Again place the dough in fridge for 30 minutes. Then bake the shell in a preheated 180ºC (356ºF) oven for 15 minutes. Cool.

Spread the filling in the cooled, baked pie shell. Peel and slice pears, then place them how you wish. Sprinkle crushed almonds on the sides. Bake again at 180ºC (356ºF) for 10 minutes. Cool. Lightly pour warm honey on top and serve.

Serves 6 to 8.

Dark Chocolate Muffins

3 eggs

7 ounces honey

⅓ pound butter

3 ounces (a piece of) dark chocolate

1 teaspoon cacao

½ pound flour

1 teaspoon baking powder

Whip eggs in a deep bowl. Add honey and butter and continue to whip. Melt chocolate in a double-boiler and add to whipped mixture. Fold in cacao, flour, and baking powder, and mix thoroughly with a wooden spoon. Pour batter into muffin cups and bake at 180ºC (356ºF) for 30 minutes. Serve warm.

Serves 6.

Muffins with Dried Fruit

½ pound dried fruit

1 cup pineapple juice

2 eggs

7 ounces honey

⅓ pound butter

10 ounces flour

1 ½ teaspoon baking powder

A pinch of salt

¼ pound sliced pineapple

Let dried fruit sit in pineapple juice overnight. In a deep bowl, whip eggs. One by one, add honey, butter, flour, baking powder, and salt, and mix thoroughly. Drain dried fruit. Fold into muffin mixture along with fresh pineapples. Pour batter into muffin cups and bake at 180°C (356°F) for 40 minutes. Cool and serve.

Serves 6.

Pumpkin Cheesecake

Crust:

2 ounces biscuits

2 tablespoons powdered hazelnut

2 tablespoons crushed hazelnut

1 ounce butter

Cheesecake:

1 pound cream cheese

¼ pound mild cream (labneh) cheese or plain yogurt

¼ pound cream

⅓ pound honey

3 eggs

1 tablespoon cornstarch

Sauce:

9 ounces fresh pumpkin

2 tablespoons water

3 tablespoons honey

Blend crust ingredients in a food processor and then press the mixture in a cheesecake pan. In a bowl, manually whip cream cheese and fold in yogurt, cream, honey, and eggs one at a time, and continue to whip. Add cornstarch and whip a few minutes more. Pour the mixture into the cheesecake pan, place the pan into a water bath, and bake at 180°C (356°F) for 40 minutes. While the cheesecake is baking, finely chop the pumpkin. Cook the pumpkin with water and honey in a medium saucepan, then blend in a blender until smooth. Let cool.

Leave the baked cheesecake in an open, cool oven for 1 day. Remove cheesecake and cut. Decorate with pumpkin sauce and serve.

Serves 8 to 10.

Dark Chocolate Pudding

2 tablespoons cocoa

5 tablespoons flour

½ cup honey

5 cups milk

½ pound bitter chocolate

Mix cocoa and flour thoroughly in a medium saucepan. Add honey and milk. Stir and heat until it boils. When it boils, remove from heat and stir in bitter chocolate. When chocolate melts, pour pudding into individual serving cups. Cool and serve.

Serves 6 to 8.

Cupcakes

Cake:
3 eggs

6 ounces honey

6 ounces butter

1 vanilla stick (pod with beans)

2 cups flour

1 tablespoon baking powder

Topping:
½ pound mild cream (labneh) cheese

3 tablespoons honey

½ cup butter

Any colorful fruit you wish

Whip eggs, honey, and butter in a deep bowl for cupcake batter. Slice and scrape the beans from inside the vanilla pod into the mixture. Stir flour and baking powder in another bowl and add into the batter. Pour the batter into muffin cups and bake at 180°C (356°F) for 35 minutes. Cool.

Blend mild cream cheese, honey, and butter in a bowl. Divide this mixture into 3, and use colorful fresh or dried fruit as coloring. Use a pastry bag to decorate the cupcakes and serve.

Serves 6 to 8.

Chocolate Risotto

½ cup rice

3 cups milk

2 oranges

½ pound bitter chocolate

2 tablespoons honey

Heat rice and milk in a medium saucepan to a boil. Then simmer on low heat for 20 more minutes, stirring occasionally. Slice the oranges in circles and sauté them in a pan, cooking both sides. Place cooked oranges at the bottom of individual serving bowls. When rice completely absorbs milk, add chocolate. When the chocolate melts, remove from heat and add honey. Spoon the risotto onto the sliced oranges and serve.

Serves 4 to 6.

Red Fruit Phyllo Baskets

1 sheet phyllo dough
1 tablespoon melted butter
10 ounces mixed red fruits
2 tablespoons honey

Brush phyllo dough with butter carefully. Fold dough in 2 and cut it in squares of 1x1 inch. Place cut dough in small muffin cups. Bake them at 180ºC (356ºF) for 15 minutes until they turn golden-brown. Stir red fruits with honey in a mixing bowl until they are coated. Once dough cools, place the fruit-honey mixture on top and serve.

Serves 4 to 6.

Molasses Peanut Mash

½ pound unsalted peanuts
½ pound molasses

Hull peanuts. Place them in a medium pan and start frying. When they turn lightly reddish, remove from heat and place in food processor. Chop them and then put into a mixing bowl. Add molasses slowly and stir and coat the crushed peanuts thoroughly and serve. (This recipe may be used for hazelnuts, too.)

Serves 8.

Tea Compote
with Dried Fruit

1 pound different kinds of dried fruit

2 cups hot water

1 Earl Grey tea bag

4 cups orange juice

Steep dried fruit in hot water and tea, in a deep bowl with a cover, for
1 hour. Drain and place into individual serving cups. Pour orange juice
over it and serve. (You may use some ice especially in summer.)

Serves 6 to 8.

Crumble

3 ounces flour

1 tablespoon coconut flakes

4 tablespoons butter

2 tablespoons honey

3 ounces red fruit

1 ounce cream

In one bowl, mix flour and coconut. In another bowl, blend butter and honey. Blend them together slowly, by hand, until it becomes a chunky mixture. Drop some mixture and dried red fruit into layers in oven cups. Drop a dollop of cream on top. Repeat these steps for every cup. Bake at 180°C (356°F) for 15 minutes. Cool and serve.

Serves 6.

Muesli with Dried Fruit and Yogurt

1 cup plain yogurt

1 tablespoon honey

1 cup muesli

4 dried figs

8 dried apricots

2 tablespoons raisins

2 tablespoons unsalted mixed nuts

1 tablespoon linseed

Blend yogurt and honey in a deep bowl. Divide it equally into 4 cups. Sprinkle muesli, dried figs and apricots, raisins, nuts, and linseed equally into each cup and serve.

Serves 4.

Muesli with Fresh Fruit and Mild Cream Cheese

½ pound mild cream (labneh) cheese
½ pound muesli
1 medium Japanese persimmon
1 medium apple
4 damson plums
4 blackberries
4 tablespoons honey

Divide mild cream cheese equally onto 4 plates. Sprinkle muesli on them. Sprinkle bits of fruits randomly on top of the muesli. Pour and decorate with honey and serve.

Serves 4.

Honey Ice Cream

18 ounces cream

6 ounces honey

Start blending cream in a deep bowl. When it starts to thicken, add honey slowly. When it thickens completely, pour in a metal bowl and place in the freezer. Remove each hour and mix well. After 4 hours, when it obtains desired thickness, serve. (Serving dishes must be cool. This is important. Make this ice cream with any fruit, by adding fruit mash with honey into ice cream.)

Serves 4 to 6.

Pineapple with Mild Cream Cheese

10 ounces mild cream (labneh) cheese
3 tablespoons honey
1 vanilla stick (pod with beans)
8 slices pineapple
5 tablespoons molasses

In a bowl, blend mild cream cheese, 1 tablespoon honey and vanilla bean paste from the pod. In another bowl, mix 2 tablespoons honey and 5 tablespoons of molasses. Lightly sauté pineapples in a medium pan for 2 minutes. Put a dollop of mild cream cheese on the bottom of individual serving plates. Place a slice of pineapple on top. Make 2 layers on each plate by repeating those steps. Pour the honey-molasses mixture on top, and serve. (Maple or date syrup may be substituted for honey and molasses. This recipe may also be varied with bananas or any other fruit.)

Serves 4.

Biscotti

4 eggs
½ pound honey
5 tablespoons butter
1 pound flour
2 teaspoons baking powder
½ teaspoon baking soda
7 ounces blueberries
3 ounces dried apricot
2 ounces peeled pistachios

Apart from dried apricot and pistachios, knead other ingredients together. Fold in pistachios and dried fruit. Divide dough into 2 equal parts. Shape them into loaves or pour in bread tins. Bake at 180ºC (356ºF) for 20 minutes. Wait one day. The next day, slice the bread and place slices on an oven tray in rows. Bake again at 150ºC (302ºF) for about 20 minutes until they are dry. Cool and serve.

Serves 6 to 8.